BOOK ANALYSIS

By Anna Scriven

The Scarlet Letter

BY NATHANIEL HAWTHORNE

NATHANIEL HAWTHORNE 9

THE SCARLET LETTER 13

SUMMARY 17

The Custom House
A public shaming
Secret identities
The vulnerable vicar
Hester takes control
A public confession

CHARACTER STUDY 25

Hester Prynne
Arthur Dimmesdale
Pearl
Roger Chillingworth
The narrator

ANALYSIS 31

The romance genre
The nature of sin
Form and style

FURTHER REFLECTION 39

FURTHER READING 43

NATHANIEL HAWTHORNE

AMERICAN NOVELIST

- **Born in Salem (USA) in 1804.**
- **Died in Plymouth (USA) in 1864.**
- **Notable works:**
  - *Twice-Told Tales* (1837), short story collection
  - *The House of the Seven Gables* (1851), novel
  - *The Blithedale Romance* (1852), novel

Nathaniel Hawthorne was born in Salem, Massachusetts, into a family that had been present in the town since its founding. He was a descendant of John Hathorne, a leading judge in the Salem Witch Trials. It is thought that Hawthorne altered the spelling of his surname to distance himself from his controversial ancestor. Hawthorne married in 1842 and had three children.

Hawthorne is famous for his psychologically complex works, most of which explore human guilt and sin. He is classed as a Romantic writer, specifically a Dark Romantic, and elements of the supernatural can be found in many of his writings. Along with his acclaimed novels, Hawthorne wrote many short stories and three nonfiction texts. He is now viewed as one of America's greatest writers and influenced writers such as Herman Melville (1819-1891) and William Faulkner (1897-1962).

THE SCARLET LETTER

AN EXPLORATION OF ADULTERY AND GUILT

- **Genre:** novel
- **Reference edition:** Hawthorne, N. (2015) *The Scarlet Letter*. UK: CreateSpace Independent Publishing Platform.
- **1st edition:** 1850
- **Themes:** love, sin, adultery, hypocrisy, guilt, virtue, isolation, justice

The Scarlet Letter is set in Boston during the 17th century and tells the tale of Hester Prynne, a woman who is forced to wear a fabric scarlet 'A' on her chest as a punishment for committing adultery. She is excluded from the Puritan society in which she lives, yet still refuses to name the father of her illegitimate child. The novel follows her story over the course of several years, examining the impact that her transgression and punishment have on her and those close to her. Hawthorne uses Hester's tale to explore ideas of virtue, justice and revenge in colonial America, reflecting on the repressive nature of society during this period.

The Scarlet Letter was one of the first mass-produced books in America and was an instant success. The novel's rich symbolism and strong female protagonist mean that it remains popular today, and it was included in *The Guardian*'s list of the top hundred novels in English in 2015.

SUMMARY

THE CUSTOM HOUSE

The novel begins with the narrator describing how he came to write the story of *The Scarlet Letter.* He explains that he discovered the fabric titular letter while working as a surveyor at the Custom House in Salem, along with a record written by a Mr Surveyor Prue, detailing events that occurred towards the end of the 17th century. The narrator decides to write a book based on this discovery after he loses his job in a political reshuffle. He admits that he has taken some liberties in recording the tale, but states that it is inspired by the truth.

A PUBLIC SHAMING

We are introduced to Hester Prynne on the day of her public punishment. We learn through the questions of an intrigued newcomer to town that she is married, but her husband has remained in Europe to study while she waited for him in America. Despite this, she has recently given birth to a daughter. As a result, she has been jailed for months and is now forced to embroider a scarlet letter 'A' on her breast as a symbol of her sin. She must stand on a scaffold in front of the entire town to show her shame, a punishment that she bravely bears. The townsmen attempt to get her to name the father of her child, pressuring the young minister Arthur Dimmesdale to speak with her. Despite his eloquent words, Hester does not name her fellow sinner.

SECRET IDENTITIES

The newcomer in town, Roger Chillingworth, is revealed to be a man of medicine and is sent to aid Hester and her ill daughter in jail. He reveals himself to be Hester's husband, finally come to join her. He asks her to reveal the name of her lover and she once again refuses. In response, he asks her to also keep his identity a secret and swears to uncover the mystery man's identity.

Hester moves out of the jail with her daughter, named Pearl, and continues to keep both men's secrets. She is shunned by the town but manages to earn a wage with her embroidery skills. Time passes, and Pearl grows up to be wilful and stubborn. Town officials consider removing her from her mother's care, fearing that she is being raised in sin, but Arthur Dimmesdale convinces them of a mother's need for her child.

THE VULNERABLE VICAR

Despite his success in helping Hester, Dimmesdale appears to be wasting away. There is no discernible cause for his illness, which appears to be psychological in origin. Chillingworth, still investigating Hester's lover, takes a great interest in the young minister and eventually moves in with him, supposedly to give him round-the-clock care. Chillingworth suspects that Dimmesdale and Hester are linked and attempts to test his theory, adding to the reverend's torment. One afternoon, as Dimmesdale sleeps, Chillingworth examines his chest, discovering a symbol on his breast (the details of which are not divulged to the reader) which confirms his suspicions. His hatred of Dimmesdale increases, and he continues to add to Dimmesdale's mental anguish.

Meanwhile, Hester's good deeds around town have earned her more respect from the inhabitants. One night, when returning home from a deathbed visit with Pearl, Hester encounters Dimmesdale, who is standing on the scaffold. He invites the two to join him on the scaffold and stands holding hands with them. Pearl asks Dimmesdale if he will acknowledge them the next day and he refuses, though he states that he will be standing with them on judgement day, fully confirming to the reader that he is Pearl's father. A meteor in the shape of a red 'A' streaks across the sky.

HESTER TAKES CONTROL

Hester can see the extent of Dimmesdale's suffering and resolves to help him however she can. She starts by confronting Chillingworth and telling him to stop tormenting Dimmesdale. He refuses, and she decides that she must tell Dimmesdale his true identity. She orchestrates a meeting with Dimmesdale in the privacy of the forest and reveals Chillingworth's evil actions. The lovers reconcile and agree to leave Boston behind. They decide to sail with Pearl to Europe and make a new life as a family there. Hester feels freed by the decision, finally letting her hair down and removing the scarlet letter from her dress. However, Pearl puts a stop to this, refusing to kiss Dimmesdale and not recognising her mother without the letter on her chest. Hester and Dimmesdale return to town, with Dimmesdale now feeling much more tempted by sin than ever before.

A PUBLIC CONFESSION

The day before they are due to leave, the town gathers to celebrate the introduction of a new governor, mirroring the gathering at the beginning of the novel. Dimmesdale gives his most eloquent sermon yet, impressing the townsfolk. Hester, however, learns that Chillingworth has booked passage on the same ship as them and is filled with fear.

Dimmesdale spots Hester and Pearl in the crowd and can no longer conceal his guilt. He mounts the scaffold and asks them to join him once again. They do and he confesses to the town, revealing his chest to all. Pearl finally grants him a kiss and he dies. The narrator states that nobody could later agree what exactly was on his chest: some claimed there was a scarlet 'A' seared there, while others said there was nothing at all.

Chillingworth is horrified to have lost his opportunity for revenge and the evil hidden within him is exposed. We are told that he dies a year later and leaves his considerable fortune to Pearl. Hester and Pearl leave for Europe and their story becomes a legend in the town.

Many years later, Hester returns to her cottage and resumes her good deeds. It appears that Pearl married and remained in Europe. By the time Hester dies, the stigma of the letter has been all but forgotten. She is buried in a grave near Dimmesdale's and the two share a headstone, which is engraved only with the letter 'A'.

CHARACTER STUDY

HESTER PRYNNE

Hester is the novel's protagonist, and becomes an outcast after her adultery is revealed. She wears the titular scarlet 'A' sewn onto her clothing throughout the novel as a symbol of her sin. Despite her supposedly sinful ways, the reader sympathises with Hester. She becomes a caring and maternal figure after her ostracization, looking after the townspeople even as they reject her. Much of her role in the novel centres around her desire to help others: she protects Dimmesdale, hides Chillingworth's identity and determinedly raises Pearl alone. By the end of the novel, the townspeople look upon the letter as a token of Hester's good nature rather than her sin. She later becomes an inspiration for other young girls who feel under pressure from the sexist society.

Hester is physically very beautiful, with "dark and abundant hair, so glossy that it threw off the sunshine with a gleam" (p. 31). However, this beauty is hidden by her clothes and a cap for much of the novel, only being revealed during her secret meeting with Dimmesdale. Although Hester is the main character, we learn very little of her motivations. Her life before her affair with Dimmesdale remains mysterious, as does her time in Europe with Pearl. It could be said that the novel is more centred around her impact on other characters than her as a person.

ARTHUR DIMMESDALE

Reverend Arthur Dimmesdale is young and has a nervous air about him. He studied in England at a prestigious university and his eloquence earns him a positive reputation in the town. However, unbeknownst to the people, he is also the father of Hester's child. This adds a certain irony to his early interactions with Hester, in which he demands that she name her lover. Dimmesdale has too strong a conscience to ignore his sin and becomes ill from the strain of his guilt. He punishes himself and frequently declares that he is a sinner in the pulpit, but the townspeople love him more for it. In fact, many believe that his final confession was merely symbolic and do not think he was truly Pearl's father. Dimmesdale appears to love Hester and is tempted to leave with her, but ultimately saves himself from sin by confessing to his crimes.

PEARL

Pearl is the young daughter of Hester and Dimmesdale, born in jail out of wedlock. Pearl grows to be a beautiful but mischievous girl, who appears to reject the religious nature of the town. Many people speculate that she is the Devil's daughter because of this. Pearl is extremely perceptive and mainly serves to question the adult characters. She quickly realises that Dimmesdale is her father and poses many questions about the nature of the symbol on her mother's chest. Her mother views her as "the scarlet letter endowed with life" (p. 58) due to her obsession with the symbol. She is critical of Dimmesdale's hypocrisy and appears wise beyond her years. When Dimmesdale finally confesses, Pearl appears to lose her otherworldly nature: she ceases to be "a messenger of anguish" (p. 142) and instead acts like "a woman" (*ibid.*).

ROGER CHILLINGWORTH

Roger Chillingworth is the assumed identity of Hester's husband, whose true name is never revealed. He is much older than Hester and married her even though he knew that she would never love him. He sent Hester ahead to America while he remained in Europe to finish his studies. Even though he is the victim of the affair, the reader feels no sympathy towards Chillingworth. As his name suggests, he is cold-hearted and becomes obsessed with revenge, befriending Dimmesdale in order to prey on him. He is the true evil of the novel and his sin is shown to be worse than Hester's. She sinned for love, whereas he sins out of hatred. Chillingworth's body even alters to reflect the darkness of his soul: he becomes "a deformed old figure with a face that haunted men's memories" (p. 98). Dimmesdale's confession is the only way for him to free himself from Chillingworth. Once Dimmesdale is revealed as Pearl's father, Chillingworth no longer has any purpose and dies, leaving his wealth to Pearl as an admission of defeat.

THE NARRATOR

The unnamed narrator of the novel introduces us to his life in the first chapters. He works at the Salem Custom House roughly 200 years after the events of the rest of the novel. While there, he discovers a manuscript of the events and decides to write a fictional account of what happened. The narrator has Puritan ancestry and feels his ancestors would be disappointed by his writing career. He appears to admire Hester's free-thinking ways. Many details of the narrator's life reflect the life of Hawthorne, who also worked in a Custom House and was descended from a judge in the Salem Witch Trials. This blurs the lines between fact and fiction, something the narrator adds to by claiming that his account can be authenticated.

ANALYSIS

THE ROMANCE GENRE

Discussions of *The Scarlet Letter* frequently focus on the exploration of sin in the novel at the expense of the romance at the centre of the text. In fact, the first edition of the text was sub-titled 'A Romance', though this had a different meaning to the common definition of romance today. The romance first became accepted as a genre in America in the decade leading up to the publication of *The Scarlet Letter*. While a novel was intended to reflect real life as closely as possible in this period, a romance involved a more imaginative, mystical interpretation of life. Hawthorne himself distinguishes a romance from a novel in the first chapter of the book. He explains that it is best to plan a romance in the moonlight as all ordinary items "are so spiritua-lised by such a light" (p. 23). For Hawthorne, the key to a romance is finding a place somewhere between the real and the imaginary, "between the real world and fairy-land" (*ibid.*). By outlining this in the introduction to his work, Hawthorne warns the reader to expect a balance between the normal and the mystical in the tale to come.

Throughout the work, we see this balance intricately laid out. Hawthorne maintains a level of ambiguity surrounding the mystical happenings in the text, never fully confirming if they occur or not. Is Chillingworth a dark sorcerer or simply a skilled scientist with evil intentions? Is the A-shaped comet a cosmic symbol of Dimmesdale's guilt or a figment of his guilty conscience? All this is left for the reader to decide. The supernatural character of the Black Man dances around the edge of the narrative, implied to influence events but never seen. The Black Man is the town's name for Satan and at various times Hester, Chillingworth, Dimmesdale and Pearl are all linked to him. The characters discuss him as if he truly exists, as they do witches. The historical fact of the Salem Witch Trials adds weight to this belief in the supernatural. The townspeople do truly believe that the mystical exists, with Hawthorne neither confirming or denying it.

THE NATURE OF SIN

The main theme of *The Scarlet Letter* is sin and its nature. We see different forms of evil in the novel, allowing us to examine the causes and impact of different sins. The most obvious sinner in the novel is Hester herself. The story begins with her receiving a very public punishment for the transgression of adultery. We are told early on that law and religion were nearly identical in this period, and this is reflected in the women of the town's discussion about Hester. One declares: "This woman has brought shame upon us all, and ought to die. Is there not law for it? Truly there is, both in the Scripture and the statute-book" (p. 31). This statement links the idea of sin with the notion of community: by sinning, Hester has brought shame upon everyone. The woman is perfectly happy for Hester to be killed for this, which strikes the modern reader as odd, given that murder is now viewed much more severely than adultery. It is worth noting, however, that both feature in the Ten Commandments. The criticism of Hester contrasts with the virtue of her actions. Hester is shown to be caring and religious, to such an extent that the people no longer view her as evil. Due to her exile, Hester gains a unique perspective on society, becoming an independent thinker. The scarlet letter gives her a "passport into regions where other women dared not tread" (p. 112) and teaches her a great deal, indicating the possibility of people learning from their mistakes. Hawthorne does caution that her isolation has also "taught her much amiss" (*ibid*.), showing that there are also disadvantages to this form of reform.

In many ways, Dimmesdale is the opposite of Hester. He has concealed his sin and remains beloved in town. Even when he tries to confess, his parishioners do not believe it. This highlights the role of gender in society's views of sin. Hester is a woman and so cannot conceal her guilt, which becomes physically apparent with her pregnancy. Dimmesdale, meanwhile, is a man who holds a position of power and is therefore unquestionable in the eyes of the people. Despite his hypocrisy, Dimmesdale is suggested to be a good man. He is horrified by the idea of sin and cannot bear his own guilt. His conscience separates him from those who are truly evil.

Of course, it is questionable whether Hawthorne classes Hester and Dimmesdale's affair as a sin at all. As stated, he portrays them in a positive light and Hester even says, "what we did had a consecration of its own" (p. 109). The use of the word consecration, meaning 'a link with the sacred', blurs the lines between religion and sin. Hawthorne appears to be questioning whether something born out of true love *can* be a sin. This contrasts with the actions of Roger Chillingworth, who is portrayed as morally corrupt, with his actions being motivated by hatred and vengeance. Perhaps it is the motivation for an action that determines whether it is sinful, not the action itself.

FORM AND STYLE

The Scarlet Letter is written from the perspective of a first-person narrator. However, the narrator does not actually play a role in the main plot of the book. As a result, Hester and the other main characters' actions are recounted in the third person. The identity of the narrator remains ambiguous: he shares many similarities with Hawthorne, but this is a purely fictional work. The text is divided into 24 chapters, along with an introduction entitled 'The Custom House'.

There are many parallels between the start and the end of the novel, giving the characters' actions a sense of inevitability. Both feature pivotal scenes on the scaffold (as does Chapter 12 in the middle of the text), and Hester ends up buried in the graveyard that is mentioned at the very start of the narrative.

Hawthorne writes in a formal style, using elevated language and complex sentence structure. The text is characterised by Hawthorne's extremely long sentences and frequent use of metaphors and similes. The clearest example of this is the scarlet letter, which is used as a metaphor for Hester herself and for sin in general. The figurative language in the text often gives an insight into the true nature of the characters. In the opening scenes, Chillingworth is compared to a snake (p. 36), which foreshadows his later villainy, whereas Hester is compared to the Virgin Mary, suggesting that she is not as evil as is being claimed.

FURTHER REFLECTION

SOME QUESTIONS TO THINK ABOUT...

- Why do you think Hester chooses to stay in Boston, despite her ostracization? Why does she choose to return from Europe at the end of the novel?
- The book is written in a style that leaves many things ambiguous, including the truth about the symbol on Dimmesdale's chest. How does this enhance the reader's experience?
- How does Hawthorne present organised religion in the novel? Does he discuss any other forms of faith or belief?
- What is the role of Mistress Hibbins in the novel? Does she share any similarities with Hester?
- Discuss the symbolism of the scarlet letter in the novel. What does it represent? How does this change over time?
- Which quotations can be used to show that Hawthorne condones the actions of Hester

and Dimmesdale? Can it be argued that he condemns them?

- *The Scarlet Letter* is a work of historical fiction, which allows Hawthorne to comment on and criticise the views of his Puritan ancestors. Which aspects of society does he criticise? Are the messages of the book still relevant today?
- Towards the end of the novel, Hester becomes an inspiration for young women who feel rejected by society. In what ways can Hester be viewed as a feminist heroine? Are there any ways in which she is not a feminist?
- *The Crucible* by Arthur Miller (American playwright, 1915-2005) depicts the events of the Salem Witch Trials, which took place in the same place as *The Scarlet Letter* a few decades later. If you have read this text, how does it compare to *The Scarlet Letter*? What is the impact of the witch trials on the narrative of *The Scarlet Letter*?

We want to hear from you!
Leave a comment on your online library
and share your favourite books on social media!

FURTHER READING

REFERENCE EDITION

- Hawthorne, N. (2015) *The Scarlet Letter*. UK:
  CreateSpace Independent Publishing Platform.

REFERENCE STUDIES

- Stubbs, J. (1968). Hawthorne's "The Scarlet Letter":
  The Theory of the Romance and the Use of the
  New England Situation. *PMLA*, 83 (5).

ADDITIONAL SOURCES

- Wineapple, B. (2004) *Hawthorne: A Life*. London:
  Random House.

ADAPTATIONS

The Scarlet Letter has inspired over ten film adaptations, along with numerous television shows, operas and plays. The best-known of these include:

- *The Scarlet Letter*. (1934) [Film]. Robert G. Vignola. Dir. USA: Larry Darmour Productions.

- *The Scarlet Letter*. (1979) [TV miniseries]. Rick Hauser. Dir. USA: WGBH.

- *Easy A*. (2010) [Film]. Will Gluck. Dir. USA: Screen Gems, Olive Bridge Entertainment.

www.brightsummaries.com

Ebook EAN: 9782808015615

Paperback EAN: 9782808015622

Legal Deposit: D/2018/12603/539

Cover: © Primento

Digital conception by Primento, the digital partner of
publishers.